Under
Acupressure

FIRST STONE

Contents

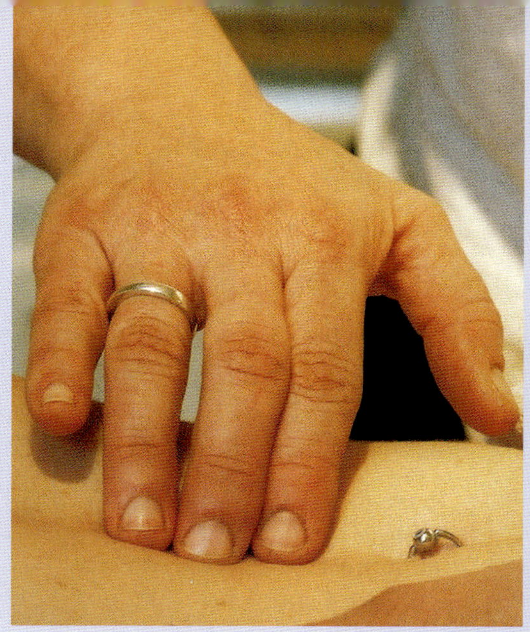

1 Introducing Acupressure

Acupressure involves applying finger pressure to specific points on the body to help restore and maintain health.

It is based on the same principles as acupuncture, and in Traditional Chinese Medicine (see Chapter Three) it may be used alone or as part of acupuncture treatment.

ORIGINS

Acupressure probably pre-dates acupuncture, making it one of the oldest healing traditions in the world. Ancient Chinese medical texts mention acupressure from about 300 BC, but it was probably in use long before this date. It appears to have been an important self-help and first-aid

> *Acupressure is one of the oldest healing traditions in the world*

technique for lay people, as well as important for physicians practising Traditional Chinese Medicine (TCM).

WHO CAN IT HELP?

Acupressure is particularly suitable for those anxious about acupuncture needles but who are attracted to the philosophy of TCM. Many acupuncturists also prefer to use acupressure with children.

Acupressure is easily learnt and can be used safely for self-help purposes. However, because its application is less direct, and therefore, less specific than that achieved with acupuncture needles, the results may also be slower and less specific. To be most effective, acupressure needs to be repeated 'little and often'.

Acupressure has been used to treat many common ailments, such as colds, flu, headaches, constipation, indigestion, nausea, earache, fatigue, stress, anxiety, and pain. It can be used for chronic conditions (such as asthma), and for tackling problems such as ME. It is also a useful first-aid technique (e.g. for fainting and shock). Acupressure has been found to be effective in rapidly halting epileptic convulsions, and it can clear blocked noses almost instantaneously.

RESEARCH FINDINGS

A wealth of good-quality research has demonstrated the success of acupuncture and acupressure in treating pain and nausea. Research also suggests that it may be a useful alternative/adjunct therapy in treating cases such as addiction problems and stroke-rehabilitation.

One area that has received a lot of attention is the use of 'acupressure bands' for nausea. These elasticated bands have a small stud on the inner surface, which, when the band is tightened, applies pressure to a specific area (or acu-point). The theory is that, if nausea is felt, pressure can be applied by tightening the band. Studies show the bands to be effective for morning sickness and nausea caused by chemotherapy.

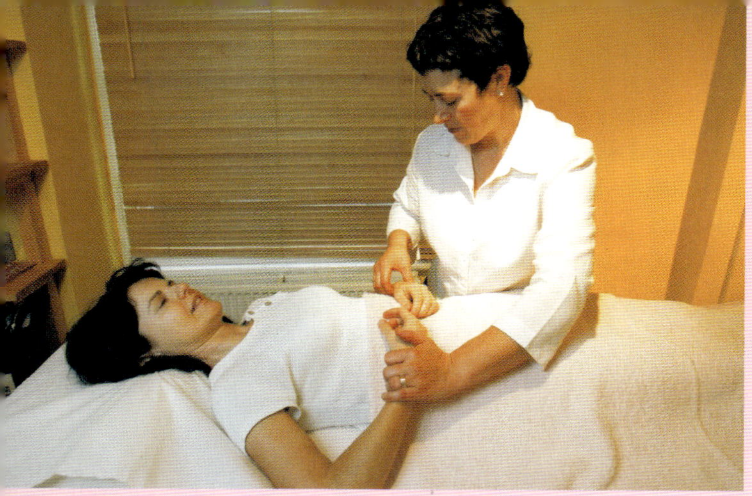

2 A Brief History

The origins of acupressure are lost in the mists of time, but it is thought that the Chinese first discovered that applying pressure to specific points on the body appeared to relieve the symptoms of many diseases and conditions.

Traditional Chinese Medicine (TCM) is based on detailed observation, and it is not hard to imagine how the tradition of acupressure might have grown out of our habit of pressing and rubbing chilled, numb or sore areas of the body with our fingers or the palm of our hand. When these observations and discoveries were made is unclear, but archaeologists have found stone acupuncture needles dating from 2500 BC.

The first written mention of acupressure is to be found in traditional Chinese medical texts dating back to 300 BC. By the 4th century AD, Chinese medicine had developed into a sophisticated and cohesive system, including the use of acupressure, acupuncture, moxibustion (burning special dried herbs over acupuncture points), massage and herbal medicine, all underpinned by a complex set of principles and theories.

As well as being an important tool of the Chinese physician, acupressure was also widely adopted as a self-help and first-aid technique by ordinary Chinese people, particularly those who could not afford the help of a physician – a situation that remains true in modern-day China.

The concepts and techniques of TCM have spread through Korea, Japan and other Far Eastern countries where they have further evolved and changed. For example, the Japanese have developed the techniques of Shiatsu ('finger pressure'), which uses a combination of massage and acupressure.

NEW DEVELOPMENTS

In recent years acupressure has been combined with other therapies to create new traditions:

- **Acuyoga:** Combines acupressure with yoga.
- **Shen Tao:** Combines the spiritual concepts of Taoism with the practical techniques of acupressure.
- **Do In:** An ancient Japanese tradition of exercises for physical and spiritual development. Today it is combined with acupressure, breathing exercises, stretches and meditations, to enhance well-being.
- **Jin Shen:** Developed in the US, this technique uses prolonged massage on acupuncture points, as well as a variety of other therapeutic techniques.
- **Reflexology:** A specialised form of massage in which varying degrees of pressure are applied to the feet, and sometimes the hands, to produce beneficial effects in other parts of the body.
- **Seated Acupressure Massage:** Popular in busy offices, this quick, stress-busting form of acupressure takes place in a specially designed, ultra-comfortable chair.

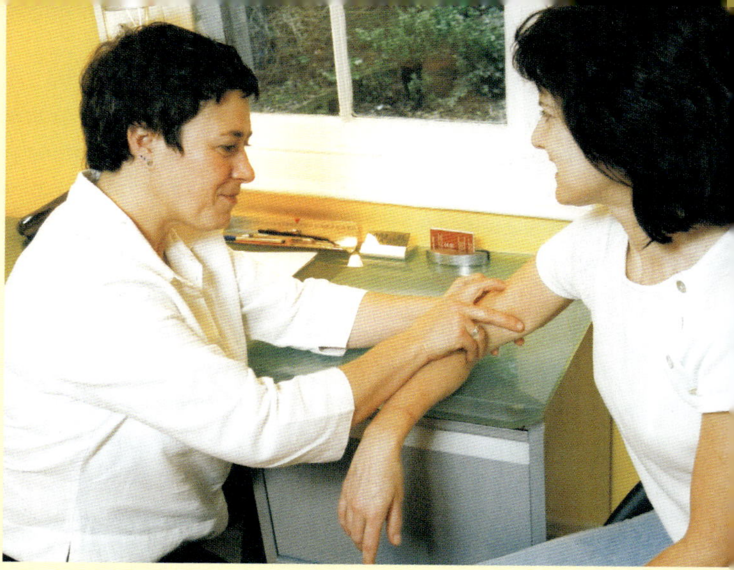

3 Traditional Chinese Medicine

In order to understand acupressure, we must first understand Traditional Chinese Medicine (TCM), on which the technique is based.

TCM is a coherent and autonomous system of thought and practice unlike anything we are used to in the West.

HOLISTIC PRINCIPLES

Chinese medicine differs from conventional Western medicine in many significant ways. For example, TCM sees the 'spirit' as an important factor in overall health, and aspects that the Western world views as important (e.g. the nervous and endocrine systems) are not part of Chinese medical theory.

The Western physician starts with a symptom, then searches for the underlying mechanism or cause of a specific disease. While the disease may affect various parts of the body, it is

◀ *Pictured left: In TCM the physician makes a detailed diagnosis tailored to the individual.*

perceived as a relatively well-defined, self-contained phenomenon. The attention of the Chinese physician, in contrast, is on the patient as an individual. The patient's symptoms are set in the context of a complete physiological and psychological profile.

The information the Chinese physician gleans from his diagnosis is woven together to form what the Chinese call a 'pattern of disharmony', describing a state of 'imbalance' in the patient's body.

INDIVIDUALITY

While two patients presenting with identical symptoms may, in Western medicine, receive the same diagnosis and treatment, the same two patients may be given very different diagnoses and treatments from a Chinese physician. This is because Chinese medicine seeks to understand how the symptoms fit into the patient's entire being. But as Ted Kapchuk, an expert in Oriental medicine, has said, "The perceptions of the two traditions reflect two different worlds, but both can affect and often heal human beings regardless of their cultural affiliation".

PRINCIPLES OF TCM

The principles of Traditional Chinese Medicine are complex and rather alien to our Western ways of thinking, but there is a logical consistency to them. Without at least some understanding of what is involved, it is impossible to really understand the nature of a technique such as acupressure.

HEAVEN AND EARTH

The Chinese believe that man lives between Heaven and Earth, two poles representing creativity and receptiveness, and givers of air (Heaven) and food (Earth). The energies of Heaven and Earth combine in us to provide life energy. This meeting of Heaven and Earth within a person must be kept in harmony and balance. Each of our internal organs has a particular function in this process, and must also work in harmony with the other organs. It is a finely-tuned system, so a problem with one organ will also affect the whole.

THE TAO (OR DAO)

The Tao ('path' or 'way') is the way we do things or the way the universe works. Living in harmony with the Tao is the essence of good health. Wisdom comes from attuning oneself more finely to the Tao.

A vital part of the Tao is the fundamental duality that exists in nature – female with male, cold and heat, etc. This dynamic system is encapsulated in the concept of Yin and Yang.

YIN AND YANG

The original meaning of the word 'Yin' was 'the shady side of the slope or the north bank of a river', while Yang meant 'the sunny side of a slope or

The Yin Yang (Tai Ji) symbol demonstrates the importance of balance.

the south bank of a river'. These meanings have been expanded to describe the delicate balance of dark (Yin) and light (Yang).

In Chinese medicine Yin/Yang is used to describe and distinguish patterns of disharmony. Reflection suggests Yin, action Yang; fast, sudden onset suggests Yang, slow and lingering conditions are Yin; under-activity is Yin, over-activity, Yang. Disharmony (ill-health) is classified into Eight Principle Patterns:

Yin	Yang
Interior	Exterior
Deficiency	Excess
Cold	Heat

However, nothing is entirely Yin or Yang, everything has within it the possibility of changing into its opposite. The Tai Ji symbol best illustrates this dynamic relationship. The dark and light are in balance, and the small circles of white and black represent the idea that nothing is pure Yin or pure Yang. The symbol also demonstrates the inter-dependence of Yin and Yang and the counterbalance between them that creates a natural tendency to bring things back to a norm (or homoeostasis).

FIVE ELEMENTS

A further refinement of Yin/Yang is the concept of the Five Elements or Phases. These are Water, Wood, Fire, Earth and Metal. Each is associated with a different season, emotions and organs (some of which are different to those we recognise in the West (see table opposite).

The Five Elements interact and influence each other and are often depicted in a circle.

THE CYCLES

The interactions between the elements are governed by the Sheng and Ke cycles (see page 20).

'Sheng' means 'to promote or engender'. In the Sheng cycle, each Element gives birth to the one following it in the circle. So Earth produces Metal, for example, and Water

THE FIVE ELEMENTS

ELEMENT	SEASON	EMOTION	ORGAN
Wood	Spring	Anger	Liver, Gallbladder
Fire	Summer	Joy	Heart, Small Intestine, Heart Protector, Triple Heater
Earth	Late summer	Pensiveness/ obsessiveness	Spleen, Stomach
Metal	Autumn	Grief	Lungs, Large Intestine
Water	Winter	Fear	Kidney, Bladder

THE FIVE ELEMENTS

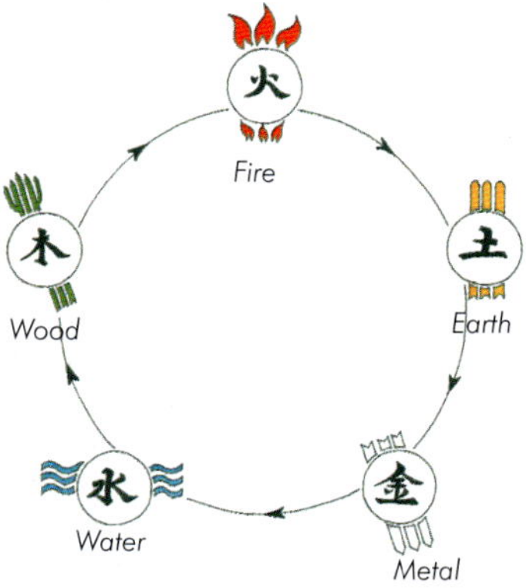

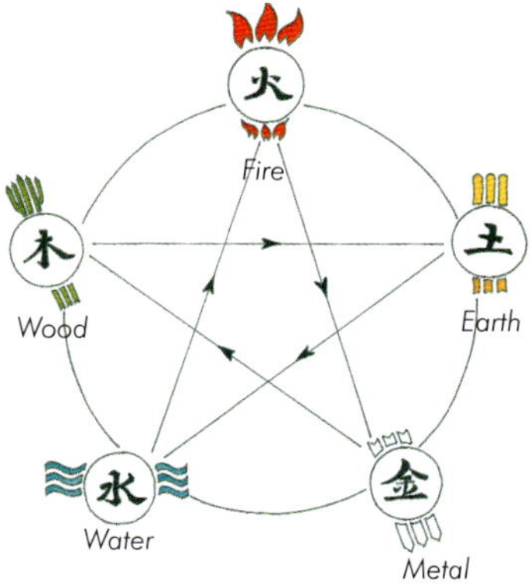

The Five Elements – Water, Metal, Wood, Fire and Earth – interact and influence each other according to the governing cycles.

produces Wood.

'Ke' means 'control' and 'restraint'. In the Ke cycle, each Element controls the next-but-one Element following it. So, Fire controls Metal, and Wood controls Earth.

The Sheng cycle and the Ke cycle must both operate together and continuously in order to maintain health. Any imbalance will disturb the whole.

There are other principles of TCM that are important (e.g. the Ten Heavenly Stems and the Eight Trigrams), but for the purposes of an introductory guide to acupressure, the principles outlined above provide a solid foundation on which an understanding of TCM can be built.

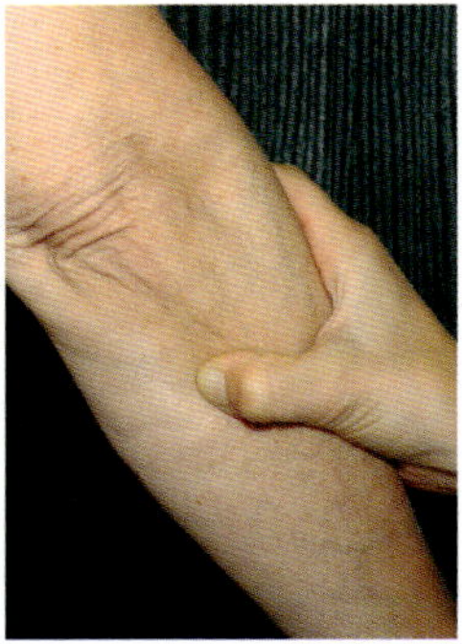

Influencing specific organs (such as the fifth Small Intestine point pictured left) helps to maintain balance in the Sheng and Ke cycles.

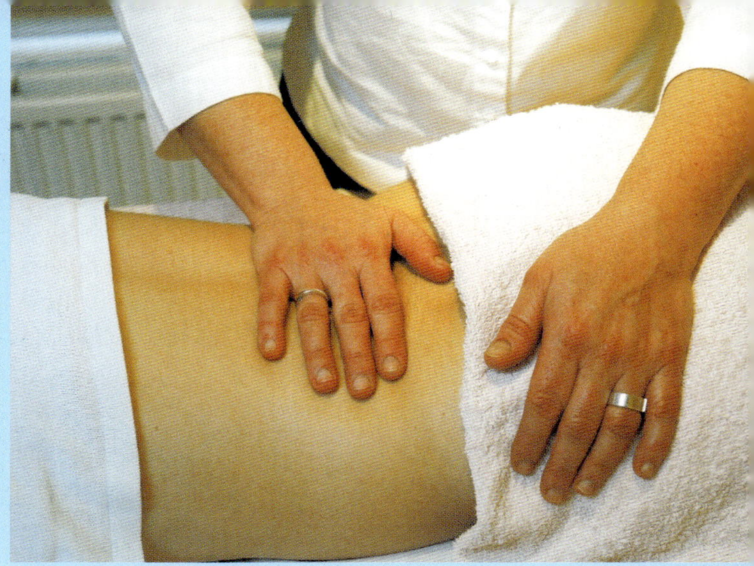

4 How Acupressure Works

Whereas acupuncture uses needles, acupressure involves the use of the fingers.

Apart from this basic difference, the way in which both techniques work is much the same. Each person is said to have Five Fundamental Aspects to their being: Jing, Qi and Shen (the Three Treasures), and Xue (Blood) and Jin-Ye (Body Fluids).

JING

This is the deep energy or 'essence' that sustains us. It is the basic power structure of the body, which determines an individual's sexual, mental and defensive energies.

QI

Qi is the life force or 'vital energy' of the body. There are different types of Qi associated with different parts of our body, each with its own qualities. 'Original Qi' relates to the Kidneys and lower back. It is responsible for the strength of the constitution. 'Defensive Qi' relates to the Lungs. It flows on the body's surface.

'Nutritive Qi' circulates continuously in the meridians (see below).

When we are healthy, the different types of Qi interact harmoniously, producing a sense of well-being. In illness, specific types of Qi may be deficient or in excess.

Qi flows in the Jing-Luo – the invisible network of meridians that cover the body.

Acupressure and acupuncture both regulate Qi by either inserting needles into one or more points along the meridians, or applying

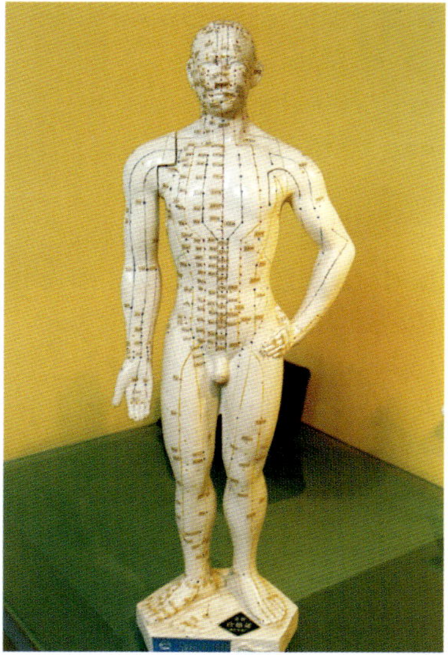

Qi flows in the Jing-Lo (meridian lines), represented on this model.

pressure to the points. The principle functions of Qi are to:

- **Activate and move:** Life is movement – breathing, eating, walking and so on. Qi governs this movement.
- **Nourish:** Qi nourishes and maintains the organs and tissues.
- **Protect:** Qi helps to build up resistance to disease.
- **Warm:** Qi produces warmth through its activity.

SHEN

Shen is the spirit energy. It relates to an individual's attitude, consciousness and the Heart. Shen gives brightness to life and depth of being, and it is affected by conditions such as depression, delirium and shock.

XUE (BLOOD)

Blood is seen as a dense form of Qi, whose function is to nourish the body. Qi is called the 'commander of the Blood', because of the role it plays in its formation, and because Qi moves Blood around the body. Blood is called the 'mother of Qi', providing nourishment to the body.

JIN-YE (BODY FLUIDS)

Body Fluids moisten and lubricate. There are two types:

- **Jin:** This is thin and watery, and responsible for moistening the skin and hair
- **Ye:** This is thicker and heavier, and lubricates the joints, sense organs, brain and spinal cord.

The balance between the Five Substances is important. Equilibrium is maintained by the Zang-Fu (the organs) and the way they function. The functions of the Zang-Fu are integrated through the body by the meridian network.

ZANG-FU (ORGANS)

The Chinese tend to focus more on the function and spheres of influence of organs, rather than their physical structure. And these spheres of influence are often much wider than the physiological functions we ascribe to the various organs in our body. The Chinese describe organs as either Zang or Fu (see page 28).

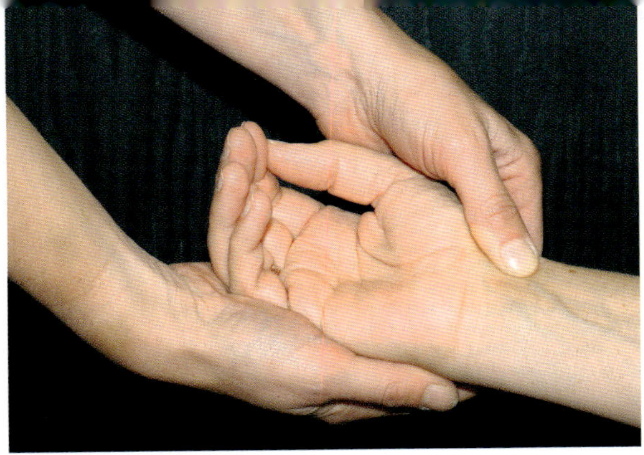

Working on acupoints H4 and H7 of the Heart meridian (Zang).

The organs, and especially the Zang organs, are responsible for processing the Five Fundamental Aspects, and it is the integrated functioning of the organs through the free-flowing movement of Qi in the Jing-Luo that maintains health.

Zang organs

These are the 'solid organs'. Zang organs are Yin because they store and preserve important substances, transform and utilise energy, and control the inner workings of the body.

ORGANS AND THEIR FUNCTIONS

ZANG ORGANS

- **Liver:** Seat of the soul, stores and controls the flow of Qi and Blood around the body.
- **Heart:** Seat of all powers of mind and soul, and controls Blood.
- **Pericardium:** Protects and assists the Heart. (Not strictly an organ, in TCM the Pericardium is 'protector of the Heart', with a strong influence on circulation and sex.)
- **Spleen:** Transforms and transports food, fluids and Qi through the body.
- **Lungs:** Rhythmic regulator, distributes Qi through the body.
- **Kidneys:** Stores Qi, governs growth and development.

FU ORGANS

- **Gall Bladder:** Stores bile, assists Liver.
- **Small Intestine:** Receives and transforms material from Stomach.
- **Triple Heater:** Protector of organs and regulator of temperature and fluid metabolism. (Not strictly an organ, the Triple Heater embraces several complex functions, including distribution of Qi.)
- **Stomach:** Extracts Qi from liquids and solids.
- **Large Intestine:** Absorbs water and nutrtients, and eliminates waste as faeces.
- **Bladder:** Accessory to Kidneys, and eliminates waste and urine.

Fu organs

These are the 'hollow organs'. The Fu organs are Yang because they are sites of activity and movement, and are involved with the transformation and elimination of impure (waste) substances.

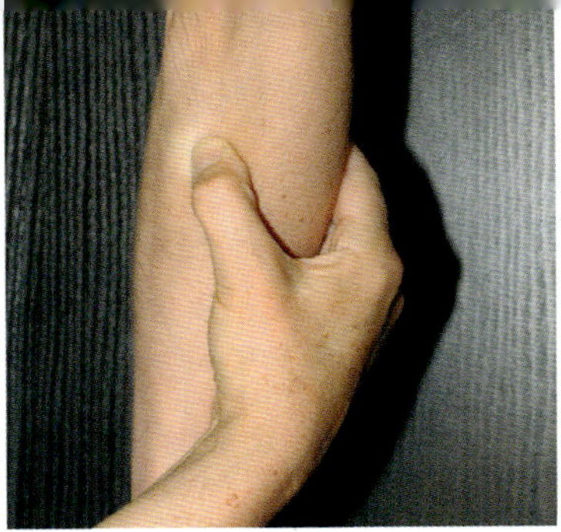

Here the practitioner is working on the Triple Heater – one of the Fu organs.

JING-LUO (MERIDIAN SYSTEM)

Meridians are pathways of energy, sometimes called channels (although this is misleading, as their anatomical existence has not been demonstrated).

The Chinese give different names to different parts of the system, according to their position and function (see table on page 30).

All meridians start or end at the hands or feet. In addition

MERIDIAN POSITIONS AND FUNCTIONS

- **Main meridians (12 pairs):** Directly connected to the organs from which they take their names. They have pathways near the surface and acupuncture points.
- **Extraordinary meridians:** Act as powerful reservoirs for the main meridians. Only two have their own 'points'.
- **'Luo' or Connecting meridians:** Join each main meridian to its paired meridian.
- **Muscle meridians:** Closer to the surface than the main meridians. They nourish muscles and joints.

to the coupling of meridians, they are also grouped according to the quality of the energy they carry. This produces another six pairs of meridians, each pair made up of one arm and one leg meridian.

Along each meridian there are places that give access to the meridians, and each has a particular influence on the Qi.

In acupressure, the fingers are used to apply pressure to specific points in order to influence Qi in a particular way.

ILL-HEALTH

In Traditional Chinese Medicine, the cause of disease may be congenital, the result of poisons, parasites, accidents, poor diet, exercise or lifestyle. Causes are also said to be either:

- **External (climatic):** Those that affect the body.
- **Internal (emotional):** Those that affect the mind and the spirit.

The Chinese believe that external causes of disease will affect only those individuals whose Qi is already compromised in some way. External causes include wind, heat, cold, damp, dryness, diet and excess sexual activity (the Chinese are firm believers that too much sex is bad for you).

Internal causes relate to the effect on a person's health of extremes or excesses of particular emotions, be it anger, joy, worry or pensiveness, grief, fear or fright.

In all things, practitioners of Chinese medicine advocate the 'middle way', avoiding extremes in order to promote health, happiness and longevity.

BA GANG (THE EIGHT PRINCIPLE PATTERNS)

The Eight Principle Patterns provide a framework for diagnosis, a way of making sense of the signs and symptoms with which a patient presents. Apart from Yin and Yang, the other six principle patterns are Interior/Exterior, Deficiency/ Excess, and Cold/Heat (see box on page 17).

Interior/Exterior

This refers to the depth of a disorder, in terms of its location. Exterior conditions arise from an external cause and are located in the superficial layers of the body. Onset is sudden. External conditions are short-lasting, affecting the superficial parts of the body and producing chills, fever, headaches or body aches.

Interior conditions are located deeper in the body and develop gradually. They are long-term disorders that affect organs, deep tissues or bones. Symptoms include changes in appetite or bowel movements, internal discomfort or pain.

Deficiency/Excess

This pattern provides an assessment of vitality and the ability to withstand disease. Deficiency shows a general emptiness, and reflects an insufficiency of Blood, Qi or Body Fluids, or the underactivity of an organ. Symptoms include a feeling of weakness, inactivity and a weak voice.

Excess shows either as a strong reaction to an external attack, or evidence of accumulation and stagnation. Symptoms include heavy and forceful movement, heavy breathing, congestion, fullness, and bloating. Pain may become worse with pressure.

Cold/Heat

The pattern of Cold/Heat gives the acupressure practitioner clues as to the nature of the disorder.

Signs of Cold include a pale complexion, slow movements, being withdrawn, wanting to curl up, feeling chilled, and lack of thirst or only wanting warm drinks. Any pain present tends to improve with warmth. Other symptoms include diarrhoea, and profuse pale urine.

Signs of Heat include a red face, fever, dislike of warmth, irritability, thirst, constipation, scant dark urine, and red skin eruptions.

SCIENTIFIC EXPLANATIONS

Western science has failed to explain in its own terms how techniques such as acupressure and acupuncture might work. That is not to say, however, that attempts have not been made.

Some scientists argue that nerve fibres carry and transmit the acupuncture/acupressure effect.

Other researchers have

suggested that the techniques work by stimulating the circulation of neuro-transmitters and other hormones (especially endorphins) in the cerebrospinal fluid and bloodstream.

There are also those who argue that the meridians are electrically distinct, and that changes within them are responsible for triggering neural and humoral (bodily fluids) responses.

However, the fact remains that, while we can see living evidence that these Chinese therapies work, we are unable to explain why for the moment.

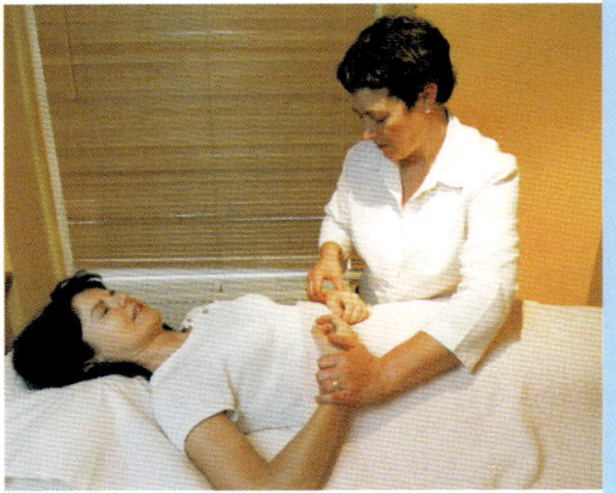

Despite the success rate of acupressure and its therapeutic value, there remains no scientific explanation for its effect.

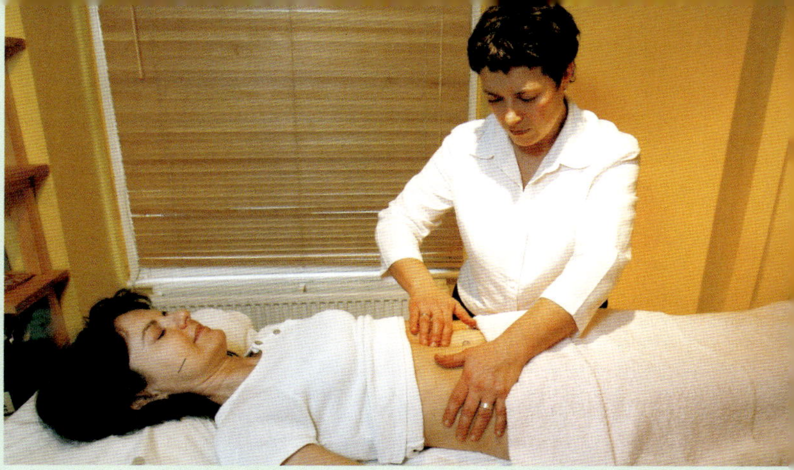

5 Will Acupressure Work For Me?

Generally, acupressure is very safe to use and receive as a treatment.

Acupressure is, first and foremost, a technique for promoting health and preventing disease. The following examples may help you to decide if acupressure could work for you.

1 HELEN

Helen is in her mid-30s. She is a nurse and on her feet throughout her shift. Although she was generally fit and well, by the end of the day she felt a tightening of her hips and buttocks, and experienced occasional spasms in these areas while at work.

Helen was concerned that, while not really very serious at the moment, without treatment the problem would get steadily worse. She mentioned it to an acupuncturist friend, who diagnosed stagnant Qi in the meridians related to her hips and buttocks. This was the result, he said, of overuse, leading to tight, sore muscles. He offered to use acupressure to treat the problem.

Using vertical elbow pressure directly to her hips, he was able to control the application of sustained direct pressure, and stretching.

Helen found the treatment uncomfortable, but was pleased with the result. Her friend taught her how to do the acupressure treatment at home using a tennis ball, and she has had no problems since.

❷ PIERRE

Pierre is 45, and a househusband responsible for the care of four children under the age of seven.

During the winter months, he has described his home as a "plague pit full of runny noses and ringing with the sound of coughs".

Pierre has built up quite a

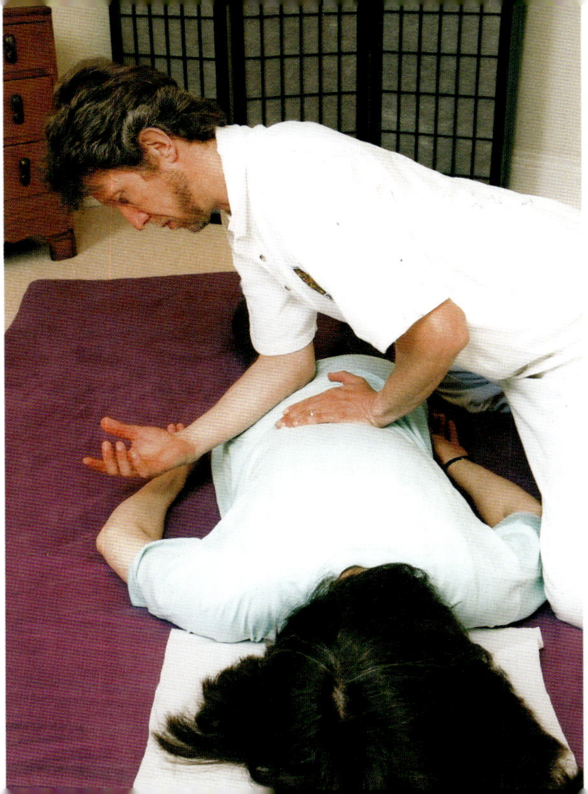

Elbow pressure applied to the hips was enough to relieve Helen's tight, sore muscles.

repertoire for treating colds and coughs, and he rates his successes with acupressure very highly. "There are a handful of points I use regularly, and the relief the children get is almost immediate. I usually give treatments in the morning, when the children are fresh from a night's sleep and don't want their symptoms to get in the way of a day's fun."

❸ JOHN

John woke up one morning three years ago and found that he could not move one side of his face. When he looked in the mirror, it appeared that one side of his face was drooping – particularly his eye and mouth.

His doctor diagnosed Bell's Palsy (paralysis of the seventh cranial nerve), and said there was little help he could offer, but that, for most people, the problem gradually cleared up on its own.

Not satisfied with this

prognosis, John visited an acupuncturist, who decided that acupressure was the most appropriate treatment. John had weekly appointments, and, several times a day, he self-treated using the acu-points recommended by his acupuncturist.

Within two months, John's face was more or less functioning normally; within six months, he was symptom-free.

While his doctor felt this could have happened anyway, John said that, during his appointments and when he was self-treating, he felt the pain ease and that he sensed his "droopiness got a little less droopy".

4 AMY

Amy was approaching 16 when she had two wisdom teeth extracted because they were impacted.

Before the operation, Amy had been in considerable pain,

but she was unwilling to rely permanently on painkillers. Then her aunt suggested she use acupressure to control the pain.

"Aunty Jane showed me how to find one acu-point on my hand and another in my jaw, which I could press if the pain got too bad. It really helped."

Amy was so impressed with the results that, after the operation to remove her wisdom teeth, she sought the help of an acupuncturist to reduce the pain and swelling. "My dentist was amazed at how quickly I recovered," recalls Amy.

❺ WHEN *NOT* TO USE ACUPRESSURE

There are only a few circumstances when acupressure may not be appropriate.

Acupressure should not be used on an open wound, inflamed or swollen areas, scar tissue, boils, blisters, rashes or varicose veins. Instead, the acu-point on the opposite side of the body should be used.

There are two acu-points that should not be used with people who have high blood pressure (acu-point GV20) or low blood pressure (acu-point K1).

Three acu-points should be avoided during pregnancy, as they may cause miscarriage (these are LI4, Sp6, B60).

Alcohol, illegal drugs, or exhaustion also preclude acupressure.

In addition, it should be remembered that acupressure is no substitute for medical treatment of a serious illness. If syptoms persist, always seek the opinion of a doctor.

> *There are few circumstances when acupressure is not appropriate*

6 Receiving a Treatment

First appointments usually last at least an hour. This is because practitioners need to make a detailed initial diagnosis.

Diagnosis involves four elements: observation, tongue diagnosis, listening and smelling, questioning, and finally, touching.

OBSERVATION

The way you walk, sit down, respond to questions, the range of your facial expressions – these will all provide your acupressure practitioner with information on the state of your 'spirit' or Shen. In particular, the practitioner will examine your facial colour – all the meridians flow to the face, so the state of Blood and Qi is evident in your colouring.

TONGUE DIAGNOSIS

The tongue is a very important source of information. Its shape, colour, coating and texture provide information on the state of the organs. A healthy tongue should be reddish with little or no 'fur'.

Tongue diagnosis is an important part of acupressure.

It should not be swollen or contracted, or have cracks on the surface or teeth marks along the edge. If you eat or drink just before your appointment, this can give a misleading picture.

LISTENING AND SMELLING

The sound of your voice and your breathing provide information on the Eight Principle Patterns (see Chapter Four). For example, a loud, assertive voice suggests a Yang pattern, whereas a weak, timid voice suggests Yin. Coarse, heavy breathing indicates an excess, whereas shallow breathing indicates deficiency.

In the West, we would be rather offended if a practitioner started to sniff us, so this diagnostic technique is rarely used in Western-practice acupressure, although traditionally, body smells and excretions are considered important.

ASKING

Your practitioner will want to get as complete a picture of you as a person as possible. As well as asking about your health problem, you will be asked to give a full medical history and a summary of your family's medical history (in case there are family patterns).

Some questions may seem rather odd (e.g. when you perspire, your reactions to heat and cold, the colour of your urine and faeces, the length of your menstrual cycle and heaviness of bleeding, your sleeping patterns, etc.), but your answers will help your practitioner to establish patterns of excess and deficiency.

TOUCHING

Your practitioner may ask to palpate areas of your body that may be painful. In this way, he or she will be able to detect heat, cold, swelling, tightness or lack of skin tone. To detect imbalances in particular organs, your practitioner may also touch specific acu-points.

THE PULSE

Taking the pulse is one of the fundamental diagnostic tools of TCM. It is important that you are relaxed for this, so if you were late or in a hurry when you arrived, you may be asked to lie for a few minutes to allow the pulse to settle.

Your practitioner will assess your balance of Qi from three positions at the wrist of each hand.

These positions correspond to the upper, middle and lower areas of the body. There are two pulses at each position, one superficial and one deep, making six pulses on each wrist, 12 in total.

The depth, speed, general quality and overall balance of the pulses give information on your internal state.

According to Chinese medicine there are 28 pulse qualities, and your acupressure

Assessing the pulse is one of the most important diagnostic tools of acupressure.

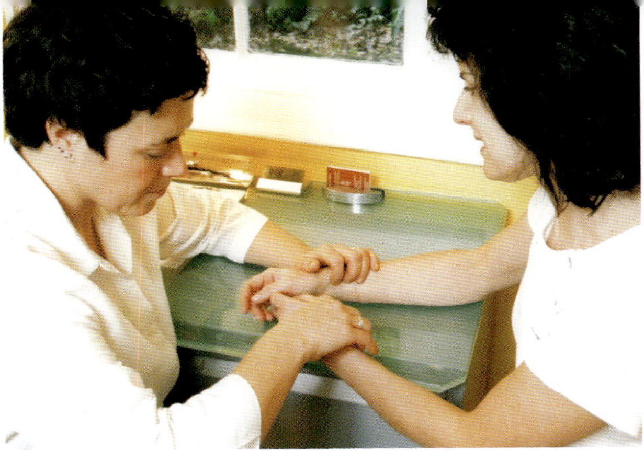

practitioner will keep all of these in mind while taking your pulse.

The qualities of the pulse can be divided into those that relate to Yin and those that relate to Ying:

Yin	**Yang**
Slow	Fast
Deep	Superficial
Choppy	Slippery
Empty	Full

PUTTING IT ALL TOGETHER

Tongue diagnosis and pulse-taking are known as the 'two pillars of the four examinations'. A sign of a well-trained practitioner is the care and attention he or she gives to these.

CAUTION

There are certain things it is best to avoid immediately before and directly after treatment because they are thought to affect Qi, and may even counteract the effects of treatment. They include:

- Alcohol or illegal drugs
- Excessive fatigue and hunger
- Large meals
- Sexual activity
- Hot baths
- Extreme emotional states.

ACUPRESSURE TREATMENT

Following diagnosis, the next step is to formulate the most appropriate treatment. This involves selecting specific acu-points to work on, and may also include dietary and exercise advice. In addition, your practitioner may also show you particular points you can work on at home.

Acupressure is usually performed while you are fully clothed. You will be asked to lie on a massage table, or on a mat on the floor. Your practitioner should make sure you are warm and comfortable. Firm, but gentle, pressure is applied to specific acu-points, usually with the practitioner's fingers, but also with the thumbs, elbows, knees and even the feet (depending on the type of acupressure practised).

You should be asked if the pressure is acceptable. If it is not, tell your practitioner immediately. How long pressure is applied to an acu-point depends on the types of pressure being applied, but it ranges from a few seconds to a couple of minutes.

Soft music may be played during treatment, and deep breathing will help you to relax. After your treatment, it is important to wrap up well and stay warm, as your body temperature often lowers during treatment.

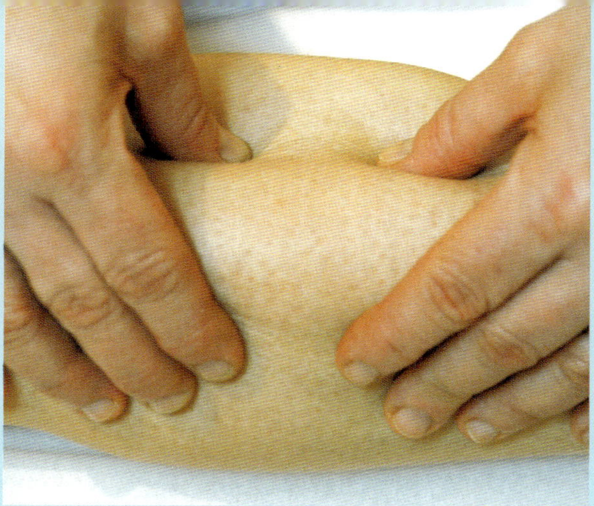

7 Using Acupressure At Home

Anyone can learn the simple, but effective, techniques of acupressure for use at home.

There are several self-help publications available, as well as practical courses for interested beginners. Together with regular practice, these will help you to develop your skills. It is only possible here to present an introduction to the techniques involved.

◀ *Pictured left: Stimulating the Bladder meridian acu-point on the back of the leg.*

TECHNIQUE

Practitioners of acupressure use not only their fingers and thumbs in a treatment, but also their elbows and even – on occasion – their feet. However, for the beginner, the only tool needed is a pair of hands.

The location of the acu-point or area you want to work on, and the sort of pressure you want to apply, will largely determine which part of the hand you use, and whether it will need support as you apply pressure.

For example, palm pressure is used both for acu-points and larger muscle groups. Your palm and fingers should be relaxed, letting the shape and contours of the muscle determine the exact hand position. Palm pressure is also used for more controlled and even pressure, in which case one palm is placed over the other, forming crossed hands.

Both thumb pressure and finger pressure are used to work on acu-points. You may or may not need to support or reinforce the digit used. Several techniques are used to do this. For example, the thumb can be supported with a relaxed fist or with your index finger. To press more firmly on an acu-point, you can also place one finger on top of the index finger and press together.

Whatever part of the hand you are using, you should keep your arms relaxed, and lean into the points to apply pressure. The acu-point may be sensitive, but the treatment should not be painful.

Before applying thumb or

palm pressure, it is often helpful to lightly pinch and pull up muscles.

Practitioners also use tapping, to increase circulation and invigorate tired muscles. First, relax your fingers, moving your wrists and elbow, then lightly tap with your palms or finger tips for 5-10 seconds.

ACU-POINTS

You should treat the recommended points on both sides of the body in order to gain the maximum benefit.

As a general rule, treat chronic problems every other day, and acute conditions twice a day, until symptoms stop.

Finding an acu-point is relatively simple. Most self-help guides provide help with this. Acu-points are usually found in the valleys of muscles and joints, and are often sensitive to finger pressure. For further details, you will need to consult a trained practitioner.

There are three different ways of stimulating acu-points:

- **Tonifying:** Used when Qi is weak, this involves applying stationary pressure with your thumb or fingertip perpendicular to the point.
- **Dispersing:** Used to treat blocked or 'stagnant' Qi, moving pressure is required, which involves moving your thumb or fingertip in a circular motion, or 'pumping' in and out.
- **Calming:** Used when Qi is overactive, use your palm to cover the acu-point, or apply light moving pressure (e.g. gentle stroking).

Whichever technique you use, apply it for 30 seconds to two minutes. When pressure is applied to an acu-point, some people experience a dull ache or a brief 'electrical' sensation. If you experience this, you can use the sensation to judge when to stop applying pressure. When the sensation ceases, it indicates that you have successfully balanced the Qi.

SIMPLE TREATMENTS

To get the most from the following treatments:

- Start with a few body

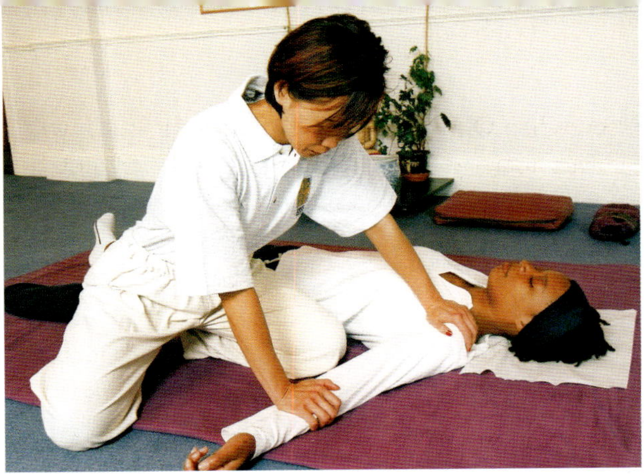

Make sure you wear loose, comfortable clothing when practising acupressure.

stretches, and take a couple of deep breaths.

- Loosen any tight clothing and find a comfortable position.
- Try to relax and let go of any mental worries.
- Avoid eating immediately before treatment, but never treat if you are very hungry.
- Warm your hands, then rub the palms together, loosen your wrists with some gentle stretches, and do a few gentle finger and hand stretches.

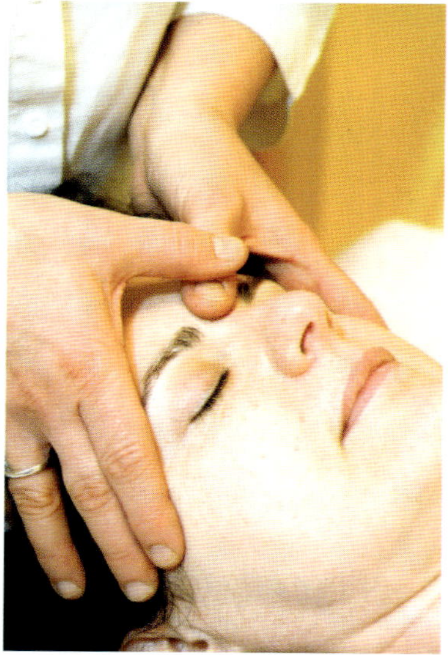

Here pressure is being applied to the Yintang acu-point to treat headache.

HEADACHE

Acupressure treatment needs to disperse the stagnant Qi in the head and regulate the Qi in the organs. Some of the acu-points that may be helpful include: GB20, Yintang, St 36 and Liv3, and LI4.

NAUSEA

There is one acu-point – Pericardium 6 – that always seems to help nausea.

COLDS

In TCM, colds signify invasion by Wind and Cold. Treatment

Here the practitioner is holding the pericardium 6 acu-points in order to relieve nausea.

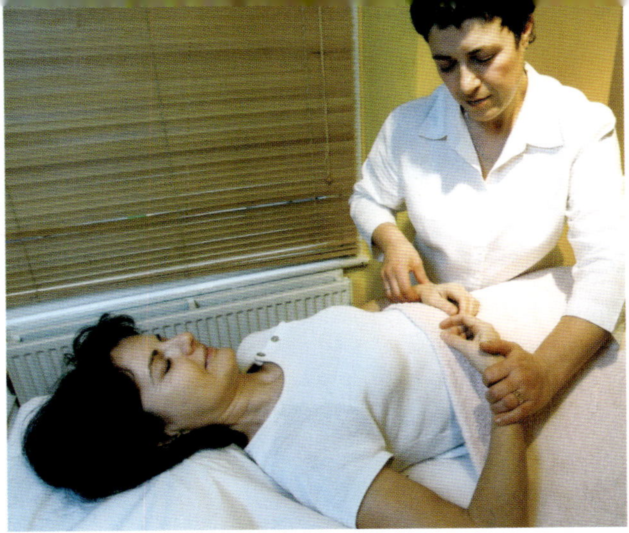

involves dispersing the Wind and Cold and strengthening the Lungs.

Acu-points that may be helpful include: GV14, Lu7, LI4 (but do not use this acu-point if you are pregnant), and GB20.

Finding a practitioner

To find an acupressure practitioner near you, contact:

The British Acupuncture Council
63 Jeddo Road
London
W12 9HQ
Tel: 020 8735 0400
Website:
www.acupuncture.org.uk
Email:
info@acupuncture.org.uk

The Shiatsu Society
Eastlands Court
St. Peter's Road
Rugby
CV21 3QP
Tel: 0845 1304560
Website: www.shiatsu.org
Email: admin@shiatsu.org

Further reading

Acupressure For Common Ailments
Chris Jarmey and John Tindall.
London: Gaia Books (1991)

Acupressure Step By Step: The Oriental Way To Health
Jacqueline Young.
London: Thorsons (1994)

Acupressure Techniques: A Self-Help Guide
Dr Julian Kenyon.
Wellingborough: Thorsons (1987)

Seated Acupressure Massage: From Ancient Art To Modern Practice, A Practical Guide For Therapists
Patricia Abercromby and Davina Thomson.
Chichester: Corpus Publishing (2001)

About the author

Joanna Trevelyan is an experienced journalist with a particular interest in complementary therapies, health and nursing, environmental health issues, and women's issues. She has written for a wide range of professional bodies, including the World Health Organisation, the Natural Medicines Society, the Parliamentary Group for Complementary and Alternative Medicine, and the Foundation for Integrated Health.

Joanna has also been the editor of the professional journal *Nursing Times*. In 1994, she was awarded a Commendation in the Medical Journalism Awards.

ACKNOWLEDGEMENTS

Thanks are due to The British Acupuncture Council (for help with photography); to practitioner Marian Fixler (portrayed in the photographs); the Shiatsu Society (for photographs on pages 39 and 57); Viv Rainsbury (for line-drawings on page 20); Patricia Abercromby and Davina Thomson (for photographs on pages 21, 27 and 29).

Other titles in the series

- Understanding Acupuncture
- Understanding The Alexander Technique
- Understanding Aromatherapy
- Understanding Bach Flower Remedies
- Understanding Echinacea
- Understanding Evening Primrose
- Understanding Feng Shui
- Understanding Fish Oils
- Understanding Garlic
- Understanding Ginseng
- Understanding Head Massage
- Understanding Kinesiology
- Understanding Lavender
- Understanding Massage
- Understanding Pilates
- Understanding Reflexology
- Understanding Reiki
- Understanding St. John's Wort
- Understanding Shiatsu
- Understanding Yoga

First published in 2004 by First Stone Publishing
PO Box 8, Lydney, Gloucestershire, GL15 6YD

The contents of this book are for information only and are not intended as a substitute for appropriate medical attention. The author and publishers admit no liability for any consequences arising from following any advice contained within this book. If you have any concerns about your health or medication, always consult your doctor.

ISBN 1 904439 16 0

Printed and bound in Hong Kong through Printworks International Ltd.